The Half Monty

by John Townsend

GINN

Published by Ginn and Company
Halley Court, Jordan Hill, Oxford OX2 8EJ
A division of Reed Educational and Professional Publishing Ltd
Telephone number for ordering **Impact**: 01865 888084

OXFORD MELBOURNE AUCKLAND JOHANNESBURG
BLANTYRE GABORONE IBADAN PORTSMOUTH (NH)
USA CHICAGO

© John Townsend 1999

All rights reserved. No part of this publication may be reproduced in any material form (including photocopying or storing it in any medium by electronic means and whether or not transiently or incidentally to some other use of this publication) without the prior written permission of the copyright owner, except in accordance with the provisions of the Copyright, Designs and Patents Act 1988 or under the terms of a licence issued by the Copyright Licensing Agency Ltd, 90 Tottenham Court Road, London W1P 9HE. Applications for the copyright owner's written permission to reproduce any part of this publication should be addressed in the first instance to the publisher.

First published 1999

2003 2002 2001 2000 99

10 9 8 7 6 5 4 3 2 1

ISBN 0 435 21232 X

Illustrations
Roger Langridge

Cover artwork
Roger Langridge

Designed by Shireen Nathoo Design

Printed and bound in Great Britain by Thompson Litho Ltd

Contents

The Characters		4
Scene One:	Monday – At School by the Lockers	6
Scene Two:	Tuesday – The School Dining Room	12
Scene Three:	Wednesday – The School Library	18
Scene Four:	Wednesday – Miss Fire's Room	22
Scene Five:	Thursday – The School Corridor	27
Scene Six:	Friday – The School Hall	32
Scene Seven:	Saturday – The School Fête	37
Scene Eight:	Saturday – Outside the Sports Centre	43

The Characters

OLLY
Olly is 14
and always broke.
Olly is best friends with Stan.

STAN
Stan is also 14 and always
broke. Olly and Stan are
often in some sort of trouble,
but they can usually talk
their way out of it.

POPPY

Poppy is friends with Olly and Stan. She never seems to be in trouble. And she always seems to have some money ...

MISS FIRE

Miss Fire is Olly, Stan and Poppy's teacher. She is organising a school trip to Disneyland Paris.

Scene One

Monday – At School by the Lockers

Olly is waiting for his friends, Poppy and Stan.

OLLY: *(To the audience)* If I told you how to get rich quick, I bet you a fiver you'd listen. The thing about money is – I've never got any. Not like my friend, Poppy. She's always got loads of it – which is very handy when I want to borrow some. Like now. Here she comes, so I'll give it a try. Just see how it's done!

(Enter Poppy.)

POPPY: Hi, Olly.

OLLY: Poppy, my petal!

POPPY: *(Sighing)* What do you want?

OLLY: *(To the audience)* I told you it was easy.

(To Poppy) You look great today.

POPPY: How much?

OLLY: Sorry?

POPPY: How much do you want to borrow?

OLLY: *(Looking shocked)* What gives you that idea?

POPPY: You spoke nicely to me. You only speak nicely to me when you want some cash.

OLLY:	Well, it's very kind of you to offer.
POPPY:	I didn't.
OLLY:	£50 would be just the job. I owe £25 to Mum, £15 to Dad and £10 to my sister. I probably owe the cat a fiver, too!
POPPY:	You could always ask Miss Fire for a loan!

(Enter Miss Fire.)

MISS FIRE:	Did I hear my name?
OLLY:	*(To the audience)* I'm just about to get Poppy round my little finger when the dragon comes along. She's the original teacher from hell. Miss Fire hasn't smiled since 1959 and she hates me. She always calls me Oliver.
MISS FIRE:	Oliver!
OLLY:	Yes, miss?
MISS FIRE:	What are you doing hanging around the lockers?
OLLY:	Just hanging around the lockers, miss.
MISS FIRE:	Up to no good, I'm sure. Now, Poppy. I've been meaning to have a word.
OLLY:	*(To the audience and imitating Miss Fire's voice)* I've been meaning to have a word … *(Then, in his normal voice)* Poppy, by the way, is teacher's pet.

POPPY: A word, Miss Fire?

MISS FIRE: Yes, about the school fête on Saturday at the new Sports Centre. Can you help me on the cake stall?

OLLY: I'm free on Saturday, miss. I've got what it takes for that sort of thing.

MISS FIRE: *(Firmly)* No, Oliver. With the cake stall, you haven't got what it takes but you'll take what it's got!

OLLY: Stan and I can sell the ice creams like last year.

MISS FIRE: No, Oliver. We want to make money, not lose it. Ah, Stanley.

(Enter Stan.)

STAN:	*(Quickly)* I didn't do it, miss.
MISS FIRE:	What?
STAN:	Er ... nothing.
OLLY:	Miss was just asking for help with the school fête.
MISS FIRE:	No, Stanley. I'm looking for someone who is good with money. Like Poppy.
POPPY:	They say it's going to be really hot on Saturday.
STAN:	Olly, we can sell ice creams again!

MISS FIRE:	No! Last year you made a loss. You two put the kiss of death on anything to do with making cash.

OLLY: *(To the audience)* So now you know what I have to put up with. The thing is, she's right. I'm hopeless with money. And I still need £50.

MISS FIRE: By the way, the £20 deposit for my trip to Disneyland Paris must be in by the end of the week.

(Exit Miss Fire.)

POPPY: I've already paid. It'll be great.

STAN: Yeah – I really want to go on that trip.

OLLY: And me. We'd have a great time.

POPPY: Then you'll just have to save up your pennies.

OLLY: Yes ... but now it's £70 I need, not £50, and in five days! It's no good, I'll have to do something *drastic*!

Scene Two

Tuesday – The School Dining Room

It is lunchtime. Olly, Stan and Poppy are in the dining room.

OLLY: *(To the audience)* Well, I've slept on my cash crisis and I've worked out how to get £20 for the trip to Disneyland Paris. I'll just have to take the bull by the horns and try.
(Calls to Poppy) Cooee! Pops!

(Poppy sits.)

POPPY: *(Crossly)* Don't call me 'Pops'.

OLLY: Don't be a stroppy Poppy.

POPPY: *(Cheering up)* Don't be a wally, Olly.

OLLY: *(To the audience)* We go through this little routine most days.

POPPY: You're off your trolley, Olly.

OLLY: You old soppy, Poppy.
(To the audience) It's no good. I'll have to ask her. *(To Poppy)* Poppy, dear …

(Stan sits.)

STAN: Poppy, dear …

POPPY: Oh no. You both want money.

OLLY: Well, the thing is …

STAN: We're slightly hard up. Broke, even.

OLLY: A small cash-flow problem …

STAN: *(Quickly)* Only till Saturday.

OLLY: And it would be so nice …

STAN: If you could lend us a bit …

OLLY: Just for a few days …

STAN: We'll pay you back …

OLLY: Just a small sum …

POPPY: £20 each.

STAN: How did you know?

OLLY: You're so clever, Poppy. And looking so well today!

POPPY: You want the deposit for the Disneyland Paris trip.

OLLY: Watch out! Here comes the dragon herself.

(Enter Miss Fire. She hears them mention the trip.)

MISS FIRE: *(Looking pleased)* The trip to Disneyland Paris is nearly full. My trips are always so popular.

STAN: We have a cash-flow problem, miss.

POPPY: More of a drip than a flow.

MISS FIRE: I must have the £20 deposit by the weekend.

OLLY: I'm working on it, miss. I'll pay by the weekend. Honest.

STAN: If you put my name down, I'll pay you tomorrow.

MISS FIRE: Oh no. Cash first. Poppy was first on the list, weren't you, Poppy?

(Exit Miss Fire.)

OLLY: *(Mimics Miss Fire)* Poppy was first on the list, weren't you, Poppy?

POPPY: I saved up. Why don't you try it?

OLLY: Saving?

POPPY: From work.

STAN: Work?

POPPY:	Baby-sitting. I do it every Friday night.
OLLY:	I'm no good at baby-sitting.
STAN:	There's nothing to it.
OLLY:	I did it once and the baby cried.
STAN:	Why?
OLLY:	I sat on it.
POPPY:	You what?
OLLY:	I thought that's what baby-sitting was!
POPPY:	You wally, Olly.
STAN:	But what about the lolly, Olly?
OLLY:	Oh yeah. What about it, Poppy? Just a loan.
POPPY:	Why don't you get a job?
OLLY:	A job?
STAN:	We did ask the man next door.

OLLY: The one with the smart car.
STAN: A red Porsche. A really cool car!
POPPY: A sports car?
STAN: Yeah. It was parked in the drive when he told us to strip all the paint off his *porch*.
POPPY: *(Groaning)* And *you* thought he told you to strip the paint off his Porsche!
OLLY: With a blow lamp and paint stripper.
STAN: He wasn't happy, I can tell you.

OLLY:	And then we asked a local builder …
STAN:	Who was putting in a new bathroom …
OLLY:	And he said to me, "Sand down the toilet."
STAN:	So we did …
OLLY:	Three bucket loads of sand.
POPPY:	Down the toilet?
OLLY:	He went wild.
POPPY:	He wanted you to sand down a wooden seat!
STAN:	How did you know?
POPPY:	Common sense.
OLLY:	Then he told me to make some cement.
STAN:	He said, "Hurry up and put that cement on the path. Be quick and step on it."
OLLY:	So I did.
STAN:	You left footprints up the path. He wasn't happy.
POPPY:	You two are just like Laurel and Hardy! Stan and Olly. Another fine mess!
STAN:	So we're still broke. We haven't got a bean for the Disneyland Paris trip.
OLLY:	*(To the audience)* So what can I do? I've got to make £70 fast. I really will have to do something *drastic!*

Scene Three

Wednesday – The School Library

Olly is alone. His jacket is hanging on a chair.

OLLY: *(To the audience)* It's now Wednesday. I've still got to find £20 for the trip – there are only two places left and just three days to pay. Here comes my only hope.

(Enter Poppy.)

OLLY: Pssst …

POPPY:	Oh, hi, Olly.
OLLY:	Pssst …
POPPY:	Do you have a problem?
OLLY:	*(Whispering)* It's a secret.
POPPY:	How exciting. What is it?
OLLY:	I need money.
POPPY:	That's hardly a secret. The whole world knows.
OLLY:	Please, Poppy. Just a loan. Just £20. Think what fun we'd have at Disneyland Paris. Just me … and you … together.
POPPY:	And Miss Fire – plus millions of others!
OLLY:	Not all the time. There'd be romantic moments!
POPPY:	So it's all the soppy stuff now, is it?
OLLY:	It's not soppy, Poppy. We'd be together, you and me, on the ferry.
POPPY:	*(Laughing)* You get seasick if it's choppy!
OLLY:	It won't be choppy, Poppy.
POPPY:	Golly, Olly. How jolly, Olly. Okay, here's the lolly, Olly.
OLLY:	A £20 note! Poppy, I love you! You're ace, you're brill, you're cool. A brand new crisp £20!
POPPY:	I'm only lending it to you until Monday.

OLLY: *(Kisses the £20 note)* What would I do without you, Poppy? You're the tops, Pops!

POPPY: Put it in your jacket and pay Miss Fire later.

(Exit Poppy.)

(Olly goes to his jacket and puts the £20 in his right-hand pocket.)

OLLY: *(To the audience)* So you see, my charm always works! And here comes Stan. I bet he hasn't got his £20.

(Enter Stan.)

STAN: How do.

OLLY: Hi. Er ... have you paid your deposit yet?

STAN: Maybe. Maybe not.

OLLY: I've got mine. A crisp £20 note!

STAN: Really? Oh, can I borrow a pen?

OLLY: Help yourself. It's in my jacket pocket on that chair.

STAN: Ta.

(Stan goes to Olly's jacket and takes the pen from the right-hand pocket.)

OLLY: *(To the audience)* I'd better not say too much. I won't rub it in that he hasn't got the money and I have.

(Stan returns.)

STAN: Are you going to the fête?

OLLY: Yeah, I want to look round the new Sports Centre. That's when it opens.

STAN: Great. Let's go together. *(Stan looks at his watch.)* Is that the time? Got to go. See you later.

(Stan rushes off.)

OLLY: *(To the audience)* Poor old Stan, always in a rush. Now all I've got to do is stroll off and find the dragon to pay my deposit!

Scene Four

Wednesday – Miss Fire's Room

It is five minutes later.
Miss Fire is at her desk when Olly strolls in.

MISS FIRE: Ah, Oliver, have you got your £20?

OLLY: Yes, miss. I hope there's a place left.

MISS FIRE: Only one. You've just made it.

OLLY: Great! Put my name down, please.

MISS FIRE: Aren't we forgetting something?

OLLY: I said 'please', miss.

MISS FIRE: No, I meant the money, Oliver.

Olly:	Here, in my ... It must be in my other pocket. Er ... it was here somewhere ... *(He desperately tries all his pockets.)*
Miss Fire:	Shall I hold you upside down and shake it out?
Olly:	*(Nervously)* No, it was here – really. I know it was. A brand new crisp £20 note.
Miss Fire:	Not another one! Stanley gave me one of those a few minutes ago.
Olly:	Who? How? When?
Miss Fire:	He ran in and gave me a nice new £20 note. He said he'd only just got it and was keen not to miss the boat.
Olly:	But ... he ... well ... it's mine ... gone ... he can't ...

Miss Fire:	How about speaking in sentences, Oliver? Then I might understand what you are trying to tell me. Have you lost the money?

OLLY: Him ... jacket ... library ... pen ... pocket ... taken ... rushed off ... I'll *kill* him ...

MISS FIRE: What you do in your own time is up to you but just remember, Oliver, that murder is against the school rules. *(She moves to the door.)* It's a shame about your money. Here's Stanley to see you. Don't be long. The bell will go soon.

(Exit Miss Fire. Enter Stan.)

STAN: Have you paid, then?

OLLY: You know I haven't, you swine. I want it back.

STAN: You want what?

OLLY: I want it now! I thought you were a friend, you thief.

STAN: Eh?

OLLY: Taking it from *my* pocket then running to the dragon to pay *your* deposit. You ... you ...

(Olly grabs hold of Stan. Enter Poppy.)

POPPY: Hey! Stop it! What are you both doing?

OLLY: Him!

STAN: Me?

OLLY: My money. It's gone!

STAN: He's gone *mad*!

POPPY: What do you sound like? This is what happens when I lend you both £20.

OLLY: *Both* of us? Each?

STAN: Yes. Poppy lent me £20 as well.

OLLY: What? So where's mine gone?

POPPY: Olly, you put it in your right-hand pocket – there.

OLLY: Yes, and it's g ... Ah. *(Looks foolish.)*

STAN: Is there a problem?

OLLY: Oops! The £20 went inside my pocket lining. It's here. I'm very sorry. I take it all back. Oh dear!

STAN: You look a bit of a fool now, don't you?

OLLY: I don't know what to say.

POPPY: You don't have to. It's given me a great idea. Fools can fool around for money! With some bowler hats and me to collect cash at the door, The Stan and Olly Show will be a sell-out! You'd better get thinking of some jokes.

(The bell goes. Exit Stan and Poppy.)

OLLY: *(To the audience)* So now I feel a bit of a fool. What's more, I've now got to write a sort of Laurel and Hardy Show. I hate acting on the stage. I'm dead shy, really. The things I have to do to make a few quid. I've got my £20 deposit, but I still owe £50 – and this will be the hardest money I've ever had to get. But let's face it, I've got to do something *drastic*!

Scene Five

Thursday – The School Corridor

Olly, Stan and Poppy are talking.

OLLY: *(To the audience)* Thursday already! I still owe money and I'm still broke. I wonder if today will bring some cash my way?

STAN: Did you hear about the raffle at Saturday's fête? Tickets are 50p and there's a £200 first prize. Who knows, it could be you!

OLLY: Just think what I could do with £200!

POPPY:	You could put it in the Disneyland Paris fund *and* pay me back.
OLLY:	That's why you're so good with money, Poppy – you don't spend it on silly things.
POPPY:	*(Laughing)* No, I just lend it to silly beggars!
OLLY:	Just think, though. If only I could win that prize draw. How many tickets are you going to buy?
POPPY:	One.
STAN:	Just one? That won't get you far.
OLLY:	I'll buy ten. Ten chances of winning £200.
POPPY:	Can you afford £5?
STAN:	It's a risk but if we win, we're laughing all the way to the bank!
POPPY:	And if you don't?
STAN:	Don't worry. Luck is on our side. I feel dead lucky today, and I've got a lucky rabbit's foot in my pocket.
OLLY:	How do you know it's lucky?
POPPY:	It didn't bring much luck for the rabbit!
STAN:	And I keep a lucky silver horseshoe in my locker.
POPPY:	There's no such thing as luck.

STAN: *(To Olly)* Stop! Hold still! There's a money spider on your neck.

OLLY: That's a good sign. The £200 must be mine!

STAN: My right hand is itching. What does that mean?

POPPY: You've got a wart?

OLLY: No, it means, "Left hand itches, money will leave, right hand itches, you will receive." Great!

STAN: There you are, Olly. Our little show tomorrow will bring in the crowds and make us rich!

(Enter Miss Fire.)

MISS FIRE: Ah, the very people I'm looking for.

OLLY: *(To the audience)* Oh heck!

MISS FIRE: Firstly, the good news. Yes, Oliver and Stanley can put their little show on the stage tomorrow. *And* I'll let you keep half the profits. Just this once.

OLLY:	That's the *good* news?
STAN:	What's the bad news, miss?
MISS FIRE:	The bad news is the trip to Disneyland Paris.
POPPY:	Don't say it's off, miss.
MISS FIRE:	Not at all, Poppy. But costs have gone up, I'm afraid. I'll need an extra £10 from you all on Monday.

OLLY:	*(To the audience)* Heck, that's all I need. I've got to win that raffle. Let's hope tomorrow is a lucky day. *(Looks at a calendar on the wall.)* Oh no, it'll be Friday the 13th! That's what I call *drastic*!

Scene Six

Friday – The School Hall

*Olly and Stan are rehearsing on the stage.
Poppy is helping.*

OLLY: *(To the audience)* Last night Stan and I went over our lines. I dread the rehearsal in front of the dragon. What a day for it, Friday the 13th!

POPPY: *(To Stan)* Hold still! You need some lipstick.

STAN: I'm not wearing lipstick!

POPPY: And a bit of blusher on your cheeks. Don't forget to waddle on when the Laurel and Hardy music plays, and trip over the bucket.
OLLY: Why don't you do this? You've got all the ideas.
POPPY: But you've got the looks! You look really funny. Just stuff that pillow down your front and fiddle with your tie and you'll look the part. Stick on your moustache ... Now put on your hat. Great!
STAN: Go on, Olly. Do the voice.
OLLY: *(Mimics Oliver Hardy)* Now that's another fine mess you've gotten us into, Stanley!

(Enter Miss Fire.)

MISS FIRE: Are you ready? Hurry up and show me how it starts.

OLLY: I say, I say, I say ... I give my hens whisky to drink each day.

STAN: Don't they get drunk?

OLLY: No – but now they lay Scotch eggs!

STAN: I say, I say, I say ... What do you get if you sit on a sheet of glass?

OLLY: I don't know, what do you get if you sit on a sheet of glass?

STAN: A pane in the backside!

OLLY: I say, Stanley ... if you had a £20 note in your right-hand trouser pocket and a £20 note in your left-hand trouser pocket, what would you have?

STAN: Somebody else's trousers!

OLLY: I'm broke only four times in the year.

STAN: Is that all? When?

OLLY: Spring, summer, autumn and winter.

STAN: I'm trying to save money but I've got a problem.

OLLY: What sort of problem?

STAN: Should I take longer steps to save shoe leather or shorter steps to save wear on my underpants?

OLLY: Hey, did you know today is Friday the 13th?

STAN: Unlucky for some.

OLLY: But I've got salt to throw over my shoulder, a black cat to tickle on the chin, a horseshoe to stroke and a four-leaf clover to kiss – and all for Miss Fire.

STAN: Oh dear. I think I got it wrong. I've just kissed a black cat and tickled Miss Fire on the chin. *(Takes a horseshoe from his pocket and throws it over his shoulder.)* I've thrown the horseshoe over my shoulder and ... *(There is the sound of smashing glass.)* Ooops!

MISS FIRE: Stop! You have just smashed one of the lights. That's it, I'm afraid. The show can't go ahead. What's more, your lucky horseshoe has cost you £15 each. Such a shame. How unlucky!

OLLY: *(To the audience)* I feel such a fool. I owe even more money now. It all adds up to £75. At least I've paid £20 towards Disneyland Paris. I'll just have to win that cash tomorrow in the raffle. I'll have to buy extra tickets. It's more *drastic* than ever!

Scene Seven

Saturday – The School Fête

On the field at the new Sports Centre.

OLLY: *(To the audience)* Saturday, the day of the fête and it's really hot. This could be the day I make my fortune with all these raffle tickets!

(Enter Stan.)

STAN: It'll soon be the prize draw. Just think of that £200!

OLLY: If I win, I'll share it with you, you know.

STAN: I'll let you into a secret. Poppy just lent me £15 to pay for that light bulb. Don't tell her, but I've spent it on 30 more raffle tickets. We must win now.

OLLY: Let me tell you a secret, too. I've done the same. She lent me £15 as well. Together we can't fail! *(They shake hands.)*

STAN: Phew, it's hot. I'm glad I've got my shorts on under these jeans.

OLLY: Me too. Sssh, here's Poppy. Don't tell her our secret.

(Enter Poppy.)

POPPY: Hi, how's it going? Miss Fire is looking for you two. She wants a bucket of water for the chief guest.

OLLY: Who's that?

POPPY: Lucky Lad! He's a racehorse and he's going to open the fête.

STAN: Lucky Lad? Then we'll have to say hello. He'll give us the luck we want. Where's the dragon, then?

POPPY: She's in the tent with the microphone. And she wants that money I gave you both for the light bulb.

MISS FIRE: *(Her voice coming over the tannoy)* Welcome to our summer fête, which Lucky Lad is about to open. Now hurry, this is your last chance to buy raffle tickets. Only one of you can be the lucky winner of £200!

STAN: I'd better go and report to her.

(Exit Stan.)

POPPY:	I'd better get back to sell cakes on her cake stall.
OLLY:	Thanks for the £15, Poppy. You'll get it all back.
MISS FIRE:	*(Over the tannoy)* Cups of tea are on sale at the cake stall. Ah, Stanley, I'm glad you popped in. I need the £15 Poppy lent you.
POPPY:	Oh no, she hasn't switched off the microphone. The crowd can all hear!
OLLY:	I don't want to hear this!
STAN:	*(Over the tannoy)* Er … well, miss er … I've sort of given it away to the school.
MISS FIRE:	*(Over the tannoy)* Really? And what about Oliver?
STAN:	So has he, miss. We spent it all on raffle tickets.
POPPY:	*(Angrily)* You what? Olly, you fools. Right, that's it! You've done it this time. I'll get you back for this.

(Exit Poppy, storming off.)

MISS FIRE:	*(Voice still over the tannoy)* And the winner of this year's Prize Draw is …
OLLY:	At least this bit should cheer me up.
MISS FIRE:	*(Over the tannoy)* Well, what a surprise. The winner is Mr Barnes, the caretaker!

OLLY: I don't believe it. I've lost the lot. I haven't won a thing!

MISS FIRE: *(Over the tannoy)* Don't forget to visit the new Sports Centre. It's got a brand new swimming pool, and much more, behind those wonderful mirrored walls.

(Enter Stan, carrying a bucket of water for Lucky Lad, the racehorse.)

STAN: Sorry about that, Olly. A fat lot of good that raffle did us. Now we're really broke.

OLLY: Another fine mess. I'll help you take that bucket over to Lucky Lad. He may give us a tip!

(Enter Poppy, still angry.)

POPPY: Oh no you don't. I've got plans for you two and that bucket. It's time for some *real* work. It's about time you earned your keep!

OLLY:	*(Nervously)* Hi, Pops. Let me explain …
POPPY:	Don't call me 'Pops'. Get to the new Sports Centre. See that shiny wall? Here are two cloths. Miss Fire says you're to clean it!
STAN:	But it's huge! We'll fry in this sun. Wait. Where are you going?
POPPY:	To put on some music – just for you.

Scene Eight

Saturday – Outside the Sports Centre

A few minutes later.

OLLY: We'll never clean all this.

STAN: It's just like a huge mirror.

OLLY: We'll just give it a quick wipe. We can do it in time to the music.

STAN: What music?

OLLY: 'You Sexy Thing'.

STAN: Thanks, but what about the music?

OLLY: Hot Chocolate.

STAN: No thanks. I've just had a coffee.

OLLY: No, stupid! The music coming over the speakers is 'You Sexy Thing' by Hot Chocolate.

STAN: Oh yeah – it's in that film, 'The Full Monty'.

OLLY: In that case, I'll take off my shirt! It's so hot.

STAN: Me too. And my jeans. This is just right for shorts.

OLLY: Just as well no one can see us. It must look like we're doing a striptease!

(They dance and mime to the music, like the strippers in 'The Full Monty'! Enter Poppy.)

POPPY: Ooh, lovely. Keep it up. Wiggle your hips and wave your shirts in the air. This beats 'The Stan and Olly Show'!

OLLY: *(Dancing wildly)* This is fun, but I'm glad only you can see us!

STAN: The music's changed.

POPPY: It's Tom Jones. 'You Can Leave Your Hat On'. It's another dancing song! Come on, do your bit.

STAN: I've already taken my baseball cap off, and I've no idea where I threw it!

POPPY: I've got it right here. And just look what's inside.

OLLY: It's full of money. Where did you get it all?

POPPY: You earned it! You've just made over £100 between you. Now you can pay me back *and* pay your other debts. You can get dressed now!

STAN: We got £100 just for cleaning a bit of wall?

POPPY: Not exactly. Have you noticed there are no people about? Guess where they are.

MISS FIRE: *(Miss Fire's voice comes over the tannoy.)* Will everyone please come back to the field. Help! Aaah! Quickly! Lucky Lad is running wild, eating my cakes and … it's just done something horrible in the lucky dip. It's getting *drastic*!

POPPY: But not as drastic as you two, eh?

STAN: Oh heck. What are you trying to tell us?

POPPY: Simple. A huge crowd just watched you strip and dance! I charged them to watch. They're going wild in there on the other side of this one-way glass and they're screaming for more!

OLLY: *(To the audience)* My first performance in the flesh! I'll never live it down. The whole school now knows my face, and my body, too! That's the naked truth! Although I made some cash at last … it was far beyond the call of duty. So there you are. Now you know the bare facts. And let's face it, you can't get more *drastic* than that!

SET A

It's Only an Animal
by Frances Usher

Runaway
by Jeremy Davies

SET B

Star Bores
by Steve Barlow and Steve Skidmore

Top of the Mops
by Julia Donaldson

SET C

The Big Time
by Jean Ure and Leonard Gregory

The Weekend War
by Tony Bradman

Sick as a Parrot
by Steve Barlow and Steve Skidmore

The Half Monty
by John Townsend

SET D

Honest
by Jon Blake

The Shadow
by Ritchie Perry

Arcade Games
by Jon Blake

Beware the Wolf
by Alan Dapré